Great Americans
John Muir

Barbara Kiely Miller

Reading consultant: Susan Nations, M.Ed., author/literacy coach/
consultant in literacy development

WEEKLY READER®
PUBLISHING

Please visit our web site at: **www.garethstevens.com**
For a free color catalog describing our list of high-quality books,
call 1-800-542-2595 (USA) or 1-800-387-3178 (Canada).

Library of Congress Cataloging-in-Publication Data

Kiely Miller, Barbara.
   John Muir / by Barbara Kiely Miller.
     p. cm. — (Great Americans)
   Includes bibliographical references and index.
   ISBN-13: 978-0-8368-8318-3 (lib. bdg.)
   ISBN-13: 978-0-8368-8325-1 (softcover)
   ISBN-10: 0-8368-8318-7 (lib. bdg.)
   ISBN-10: 0-8368-8325-X (softcover)
   1. Muir, John, 1838-1914. 2. Conservationists—United States—Biography—Juvenile literature. 3. Naturalists—United States—Biography—Juvenile literature. I. Title.
   QH31.M78K54   2007
   333.72092—dc22   2007012640

This edition first published in 2008 by
Weekly Reader® Books
An imprint of Gareth Stevens Publishing
1 Reader's Digest Road
Pleasantville, NY 10570-7000 USA

Copyright © 2008 by Gareth Stevens, Inc.

Managing editor: Valerie J. Weber
Art direction: Tammy West
Cover design and page layout: Charlie Dahl
Picture research: Sabrina Crewe
Production: Jessica Yanke

Picture credits: Cover, title page John Muir National Historic Site; pp. 5, 17 Library of Congress; p. 6 Chris Krievs (Krievs Photography); p. 7 Wisconsin Historical Society #42719; p. 8 Wisconsin Historical Society #10983; p. 9 Wisconsin Historical Society #1946; p. 11 © Michael S. Lewis/Corbis; p. 12 © Galen Rowell/Corbis; p. 13 Charlie Dahl/© Gareth Stevens, Inc.; p. 14 Sequoia National Park; p. 15 Courtesy National Park Service Museum Management Program and John Muir National Historic Site; p. 16 Wisconsin Historical Society #4392; p. 19 © Corbis; p. 20 © John Decker/Sacramento Bee/ZUMA/Corbis; p. 21 © Terry Husebye/Getty Images.

All rights reserved. No part of this book may be reproduced, stored in a retrieval system, or transmitted in any form or by any means, electronic, mechanical, photocopying, recording, or otherwise, without the prior written permission of the copyright holder.

Printed in the United States of America

1 2 3 4 5 6 7 8 9 11 10 09 08 07

Table of Contents

Chapter 1: A Young Nature Lover 4

Chapter 2: The Father of National Parks 10

Chapter 3: Teaching the World 18

Glossary 22

For More Information 23

Index 24

Cover and title page: John Muir was an explorer and writer who worked to protect and save the United States's wilderness. He founded the Sierra Club, the oldest environmental group in the United States.

Chapter 1

A Young Nature Lover

John Muir (myoor) guided President Theodore Roosevelt to a rocky ledge high above Yosemite (yo-SEH-muh-tee) Valley. Giant pine trees covered the valley floor. The snowy peaks of the Sierra Nevada surrounded them. Behind them, a rushing waterfall dropped hundreds of feet. Muir spread his arms wide. This wild and beautiful place must be protected, he told the president.

Roosevelt knew Muir was right. He would later sign a law making Yosemite Valley a part of Yosemite National Park. Muir also told Roosevelt about his plan for a system of national parks. Muir and his ideas guided presidents and thousands of others. He showed that one person can help protect the wild places on Earth.

From Glacier Point, John Muir (*right*) and President Theodore Roosevelt (*left*) had a wide view of beautiful Yosemite Valley.

5

John Muir's love of the outdoors began when he was a boy. He was born on April 21, 1838, in Scotland in Great Britain. When he was eleven years old, his family moved to central Wisconsin to start a farm. John cut down trees, dug through hard ground for a well, and plowed the fields with an ox.

As a boy, Muir loved watching birds. This statue of him stands in his hometown of Dunbar, Scotland.

John liked playing in the nearby woods, meadows, and lake. He studied everything he saw, from the tall trees to tiny insects buzzing in the air. Because John worked on the farm, he could not go to school. Instead he woke up at one o'clock every morning to read.

This brick farmhouse near Portage, Wisconsin, was the Muir home. Although his father also grew wheat, corn, and potatoes, Muir's favorite crop was watermelons!

When he was twenty-two, Muir started college. He took science classes, learning about plants, animals, and the natural world. After three years, Muir was ready to explore nature on his own. He walked hundreds of miles through Wisconsin, Iowa, Illinois, and Canada.

Muir invented and built many unusual clocks. During college, he made this clock-desk that opened his books.

In 1867, Muir was fixing a machine in Indiana when he poked himself in the right eye. He lost his sight in both eyes for several months. When the bandages came off, Muir decided to spend his life looking at the world's forests, lakes, and mountains. He started by walking 1,000 miles (1,600 kilometers) from Indiana to the Gulf of Mexico! Then he headed to California.

Muir sailed first to Cuba and then through the Panama Canal in Central America. He was about thirty years old when he reached California.

Chapter 2

The Father of National Parks

In the spring of 1868, John Muir visited Yosemite Valley for the first time. Located east of San Francisco, it is tucked into the Sierra Nevadas. This mountain range stretches from north to south in eastern California. In 1869, Muir moved to Yosemite and spent the summer herding sheep in the mountains. Later, he worked at a sawmill.

Muir learned all he could about the land around him. He began to believe that sheep farmers and lumbermen were destroying Yosemite's beauty. Grazing sheep ate or flattened all the flowers and shrubs in the meadows. Cutting trees for lumber or to make pastures left ugly, bare hills and land.

The Merced River flows through Yosemite Valley. El Capitan is the name of the famous rock formation on the left. Standing 3,000 feet (900 meters) high, it is a favorite of expert rock climbers.

In 1889, Muir and his friend Robert U. Johnson went camping in Yosemite. They talked about how to protect and **preserve** the wilderness.

Muir began to write articles about the Sierras. He also told people how forests in the United States were being destroyed. Johnson printed the articles in his famous magazine.

While camping in Tuolumne Meadow, Muir and Johnson agreed to protect Yosemite.

The two men gave speeches and talked to the government about creating a national park in California. In 1890, Congress passed a law that set aside land for Yosemite National Park. Yosemite Valley, however, was not included in it. Congress also set aside land for Sequoia National Park. This park has trees that are three thousand years old!

Yosemite, Sequoia, and Kings Canyon National Parks are in the Sierra Nevada range.

13

The next year, Congress passed a law creating national forests that could not be cut down. Many businesses and people were against this. They wanted to harvest trees to sell the lumber or clear land for mining in these forests. Muir argued that people needed forests and other wild places to visit.

The forest in Sequoia National Park has the world's tallest tree. It is as tall as a twenty-seven-story building!

Muir and many of his friends were **conservationists** working to protect nature. In 1892, they formed the Sierra Club. They wanted to make sure that the new national parks were protected. Muir became the club's first president and held this job the rest of his life.

Muir (*second from left*) led other Sierra Club members as they explored Yosemite and the Sierras.

In 1901, the Sierra Club began taking people on yearly trips to Yosemite. The first group of ninety-seven people included John Muir and his two daughters. Muir was a great teacher. His excitement about the outdoors soon spread to others.

When they were older, Wanda (*left*) and Helen Muir camped with their father in Yosemite.

Two years later, Muir invited President Theodore Roosevelt to visit Yosemite. For three days, they camped in Yosemite Valley. Roosevelt liked Muir's ideas about conservation, or saving wild areas. As president, he set aside land for five national parks, 150 national forests, and fifty-five bird and animal **reserves**.

During his visit in 1903, President Roosevelt took a ride to Inspiration Point, which rises over Yosemite Valley. Roosevelt looks out from the back seat in this photo.

Chapter 3

Teaching the World

Although Yosemite was his favorite place, John Muir explored other wilderness areas, too. In 1879, he made the first of many trips to Alaska, where he explored and drew maps of Glacier Bay. One of the bay's giant glaciers was named after him. Muir also traveled through Europe, Asia, Australia, South America, and Africa.

Whenever he traveled, Muir learned all he could about his surroundings. Then he shared his adventures and discoveries with others. During his lifetime, Muir wrote more than three hundred articles about nature. He also wrote ten books. They included stories about his childhood, his travels, and the mountains.

This photo from 1897 shows only part of Muir Glacier, which is about 2 miles (3.2 kilometers) wide. Located in southeastern Alaska, Glacier Bay became a national park in 1980.

John Muir died on December 24, 1914 at age seventy-six. Before and after his death, he received many honors. Hiking trails and forests bear his name. In 1976, the California Historical Society voted him "The Greatest Californian."

On January 31, 2005, California governor Arnold Schwarzenegger and his wife, Maria Shriver, show off the state's new quarter. The coin has images of John Muir and Yosemite Valley.

John Muir remains an example for everyone who cares about Earth. We play in national parks and wilderness areas he fought for. His work guides people who are fighting climate changes or saving wild places. As Muir himself pointed out, "There is a love of wild nature in everybody."

About 4 million people visit Yosemite National Park each year. These hikers stop to look at its amazing beauty.

Glossary

college — a school that many students go to after high school

conservationists — people who work to preserve and protect Earth and its natural resources

crops — plants that are grown and harvested for sale

explore — to travel through an unknown or foreign place for the purpose of discovery and adventure

glacier — a huge body of ice

grazing — feeding on growing grass and other plants

historical — concerned with events in history, or the past

lumbermen — people who cut down trees or who make and sell the boards that come from trees

plowed — turned over the soil using a piece of equipment called a plow

preserve — to protect something from being destroyed, injured, or spoiled

reserves — areas of land set aside for a specific purpose

sawmill — a place where lumber, or cut trees, is sawn into boards

For More Information

Books

John Muir. Discover Someone Who Made a Difference (series). David Armentrout and Patricia Armentrout (Rourke Publishing)

John Muir. Rookie Biographies (series). Wil Mara (Children's Press)

John Muir and Stickeen: An Icy Adventure with a No-Good Dog. Julie Dunlap and Marybeth Lorbiecki (Northword Press)

Yosemite National Park. National Parks (series). Mike Graf (Capstone Press)

Web Sites

Harcourt Multimedia Biographies — John Muir
www.harcourtschool.com/activity/biographies/muir
Information on the life of John Muir.

Yosemite at a Glance
www.nps.gov/archive/yose/education/glance/glance.htm
Learn about the mountains, animals, and history of Yosemite.

Publisher's note to educators and parents: Our editors have carefully reviewed these Web sites to ensure that they are suitable for children. Many Web sites change frequently, however, and we cannot guarantee that a site's future contents will continue to meet our high standards of quality and educational value. Be advised that children should be closely supervised whenever they access the Internet.

Index

Alaska 18

California 9, 10, 13
camping 12, 16, 17
conversationists 15, 17

exploring 8, 18, 19

farming 6, 7
forests 9, 12, 14

inventions 8

mountains 4, 9, 10, 19

national forests 14, 17
national parks 5, 13, 15, 17, 19, 21

preservation 12
presidents 4, 5

reserves 17
Roosevelt, Theodore 4, 5, 17

school 7, 8
Scotland 6
Sequoia National Park 13, 14
Sierra Club 15, 16

Sierra Nevada 4, 10, 12, 13

trees 4, 6, 7, 11, 13, 14

walks 8, 9
Wisconsin 6, 7, 8
writing 12, 19

Yosemite National Park 5, 13, 15, 21
Yosemite Valley 4, 5, 10, 11, 12, 13, 16, 17, 18

About the Author

Barbara Kiely Miller is an editor and writer of educational books for children. She has a degree in creative writing from the University of Wisconsin–Milwaukee. Barbara lives in Shorewood, Wisconsin, with her husband and their two cats Ruby and Sophie. When she is not writing or reading books, Barbara enjoys photography, bicycling, and gardening.